Twentieth-Century Piano Classics

Igor Stravinsky
Arnold Schoenberg
Paul Hindemith

Introduction by
ROBERT RIMM

DOVER PUBLICATIONS, INC.
Mineola, New York

Bibliographical Note

This Dover edition, first published in 1999, is a new compilation of eight works originally published separately. Igor Stravinsky's *Trois Mouvements de Pétrouchka* was originally published by Boosey & Hawkes, London, 1922; and his *Rag Time, Piano-Rag-music* and *Les Cinq Doigts: 8 Pièces [Mélodies] Très Faciles sur 5 Notes* were originally published by J. & W. Chester Ltd., London, in 1918, 1920 and 1921, respectively.

Arnold Schoenberg's works were originally published by Universal-Edition A.G., Wien [Vienna] as follows: *Drei Klavierstücke, Op. 11*, 1910; *Sechs kleine Klavierstücke, Op. 19*, 1913; and *Kammersymphonie für 15 Soloinstrumente, Op. 9: für Klavier zu 2 Händen gesetzt von Eduard Steuermann*, 1922. Paul Hindemith's *1922: Suite für Klavier* was originally published by B. Schott's Söhne, Mainz, 1922.

The list of contents and glossary are newly added. Robert Rimm's introductory notes were written specially for this edition. Translations were prepared with the kind assistance of Stanley Appelbaum.

International Standard Book Number: 0-486-40623-7

Manufactured in the United States of America
Dover Publications, Inc., 31 East 2nd Street, Mineola, N.Y. 11501

CONTENTS

INTRODUCTION

"Modernism." "Atonality." "Neoclassicism." These limiting categories cannot fully place three composers whose collective body of work at once embraces and defies such boundaries. Presenting Stravinsky, Schoenberg and Hindemith in one volume offers a pointed look at a triad of strong-willed personalities instrumental to a seminal era in music history. These three—together with Scriabin, Prokofiev and Bartók—led the evolution of 20th-century piano music, set up by the timbral and structural experiments of Debussy and late Liszt. What emerged was an elemental shift in the paradigm of accepted musical conventions. The piano was key to the *oeuvre* of all three. Though less accomplished on the instrument than such composer-pianists as Rachmaninov or Medtner, each used the piano, most often percussively, as an integral part of the compositional process.

As creators of new directions, the composers in this collection knew the importance of their theories and were published extensively. The valuable writings that resulted, in German, French and English, form a library of strategic musical tactics unique to the early 20th century. The levers of logic and intellect, combined with collateral anti-Romantic sentiments, created the basis for the provocative innovations in these pages. Though pioneers, each man felt the weight of his forebears, despite putative assumptions that all three disregarded tradition.

Arnold Schoenberg (1874–1951), presumed heir to Wagner and Richard Strauss, was largely self-taught and followed his own path without what he considered the overbearing burdens of a mentor. His works sprung fully from the traditions of German music; he considered his primary teachers to be Bach and Mozart. In a credo on the imperatives of tradition, Schoenberg revealed: "One must have grasped, admired and marveled at the mysterious wonders of our tonal harmony, the unbelievably delicate balance of its architectural values and its cabalistic mathematics as *I* have, in order to feel, when one no longer has need of them, that one requires new means."

Leaving behind the lush Wagnerian atmosphere of *Verklärte Nacht* (1899)—Schoenberg's *fin de siècle* farewell to late Romanticism—the composer gradually became impatient with prevailing musical expressions of harmony, which left his larger compositional goals unslaked. He felt that his expressive style had resolutely established itself in 1906 with the First Chamber Symphony, Op. 9, scored for the disparate ensemble of ten winds and five solo strings. This work, here transcribed by the composer's student and close friend, Eduard Steuermann, was pivotal in Schoenberg's transition to a disavowal of tonal harmony. Not quite atonal, its polyphonic guile lends itself to transcription for solo piano, in a score that deftly reveals its musical outlines to us. The important stylistic developments demonstrated in the Chamber Symphony inevitably led to the atonality of the *Three Piano Pieces*, Op. 11, composed three years later.

"The more art is controlled, limited, worked over, the more it is free," declared Igor Stravinsky. These words, perceptive beyond the limits of casual reasoning, could well be applied to Schoenberg's aphoristic piano pieces. Schoenberg said as much in a letter to Busoni: "My music must be *brief*. Concise!" This is borne out by the interior drama and brevity of his Op. 11 and the *Six Little Piano Pieces*, Op. 19, both written before he completely worked out his serial techniques. Schoenberg's move toward atonality was no mere compositional gambit. His many letters of this period display a man with single-minded, well-nigh obsessive, musical conviction. Stravinsky picked this up just by looking at him, remarking, "His eyes were protuberant and explosive, and the whole force of the man was in them."

In 1908, on the cusp of composing his Op. 11, Schoenberg wrote, "I am conscious of having removed all the traces of a past esthetic . . ." Though among the first great openly atonal works, the *Three Piano Pieces* trace a link with Brahms' intense and introspective late piano works. (The bonds of these two German composers are further demonstrated in Schoenberg's fascinating orchestration of Brahms' G minor Piano Quartet.)

The *Six Little Piano Pieces*, Op. 19, are little in name only. To be sure, the longest lasts for barely over a minute, but with spare precision they express volumes. The piano literature knows few equivalents, though Scriabin's late Op. 74 Preludes—written three years afterward—share with Op. 19 an austere concentration. Schoenberg wrote the last of the Op. 19 pieces in June 1911 as a private homage to Gustav Mahler, his devoted friend and supporter, who had died a month earlier.

An important aside seems appropriate at this point—namely, a word about neoclassicism (specifically

Schoenberg's journey in his Op. 25), a term that applies equally well to literature, art and architecture. These cultural stimulations were explored in depth by all three composers represented in this volume.

Neoclassicism adopts characteristics of 17th- and 18th-century forms, more often than not as a backlash to the emotive Romanticism so popular in the late 19th century; Bach's contrapuntal argument and spare Baroque instrumentation are magnets. Though neoclassical works generally emerge from tonality, it may be argued that Schoenberg's aims in his *Suite for Piano*, Op. 25 (not in the present compilation) were distinctly neoclassicist within the framework of atonality. This work of 1921–23 looks back to 18th-century dance forms: its movements' names derive straight from Bach's suites, with Brahms-like use of a central *Intermezzo*. Yet Schoenberg (who admired few of his contemporaries) reserved acid words for both Stravinsky's neoclassicism and the neo-Baroque style of Paul Hindemith. As they went their own way, it was not *his* way.

Arnold Schoenberg and Igor Stravinsky (1882–1971) shared preferences for clear, dry sound forms and a cultivated avoidance of plush melodic lines. We may be surprised, then, that Stravinsky adored Tchaikovsky's music, though these Russians shared a common heritage and love of ballet. Stravinsky, in fact, came to world prominence with three early ballets: *The Firebird, Petrushka* and *The Rite of Spring*. But *Petrushka*, composed in 1910–11, had a dual personality: a dazzling ballet on stage, the music itself was conceived by its composer as a *concertante* work for piano and orchestra. "The piano would play the most important part," he wrote.

It is particularly appropriate that the *Three Movements from Petrushka* joins *Piano-Rag-music* in this edition, for Arthur Rubinstein inspired them both. Stravinsky had written the latter music for Rubinstein, hoping that the celebrated pianist would put it on his worldwide programs. It did not happen. "Your piece is written for percussion rather than for my kind of piano," said pianist to composer, who countered, "The piano is nothing but a utility instrument and it sounds right only as percussion."*

At that point, Rubinstein played from memory scenes from *Petrushka*, employing the pedal combined with his golden sound. Stravinsky suddenly became enamored with the possibilities and promised to write a sonata for him based on the ballet's materials. Though not formally labeled a sonata, the *Three Movements from Petrushka* has since become one of the most beloved piano works in the repertoire, with pedal and percussive effects in brilliant coexistence.

At other ends of the stylistic spectrum, in addition to *Piano-Rag-music*, are Stravinsky's *Ragtime* and *The Five Fingers*. Partly influenced by Russian folk melodies and by jazz, Stravinsky borrowed sharply accented jazz rhythms for both *Ragtime* and *Piano-Rag-music*, exploiting syncopation above pure ragtime style. The "eight very easy melodies" of his *Five Fingers*—a very different sort of music, to be sure—still take advantage of the piano's percussive aspects as well as syncopated melodic lines.

In 1913—two years after *Petrushka* and five before *Ragtime*—Stravinsky caused a revolution with *The Rite of Spring* and became the avatar of modernism. Yet he hated that term, a sobriquet frequently ascribed to his work. He refused to be classified. Following the ballets, his works generally evolved with the more precise, lean style from which his neoclassicism arose in the period after 1920. He thus drifted closer to Schoenberg's aesthetic and even bypassed Hindemith by exploring serial techniques three years after Schoenberg's death.

Responding to a poll taken in his day that showed Beethoven to be the composer most in demand in the United States, Stravinsky opined, "On that basis one can say that Beethoven is very modern and that a composer of such manifest importance as Paul Hindemith is not modern at all, since the list of winners does not even mention his name."

While Nazi Germany would label his music "degenerate," Hindemith (1895–1963) was generally recognized as the most important German composer of the 1920s. Before the advent of World War II he came to the United States, forced out of his country—as were Stravinsky and Schoenberg before him—by European political upheavals. Though Hindemith never left tonality, the sharp dissonance in his music, however logically developed, often casts an impression of atonality. In common with Schoenberg, he considered Bach to be his true teacher, but he expressed impatience with the theories of both Schoenberg and Stravinsky.

Hindemith's use of old forms branded him neo-Baroque. On the other hand his music can seem difficult, at least on its surface, but his contrapuntal abilities and ideas reveal a vibrant creative force. Widely acknowledged then and now as an extraordinary compositional artisan, Hindemith—who played many orchestral instruments with great facility—wrote sharp, virtuosic works appealing to soloist and ensemble player alike.

Hindemith came to reject late Romanticism earlier than Schoenberg had, though both studied Brahms and each felt secure in his own style. The music of both men is rigorously thought out and displays a lack of sentimentality. Both, too, went beyond music's traditional major/minor functions to focus on the twelve tones individually.

*Rubinstein, *My Many Years*. Knopf, New York, 1980.

However, while Schoenberg embraced a new atonal language, Hindemith espoused tonality, depite dissonances that often sound atonal.

Each work in this volume emanates from pivotal points in its composer's career. Unlike Shostakovich's 12th Symphony, for example—subtitled "The Year 1917 (dedicated to the memory of Lenin)"—Hindemith's *Suite '1922'* was not named to memorialize a public event. He named that year due to its importance in his own life: a productive time of touring, performing and the completion of a dozen important works including his Third String Quartet, the song cycle *Das Marienleben* and, coincidentally, *Kammermusik No. 1* [Chamber Music] for small orchestra, composed the same year Schoenberg orchestrated his First Chamber Symphony. Schoenberg may well have given the title "Three Piano Pieces 1909" to his Op. 11 to mark a similarly ground-breaking year.

Of the five movements in *Suite '1922'*, "Shimmy" and "Boston" stylized popular American dance music in their evocations of the foxtrot and of the slow waltz named for that city. In the last movement, called "Ragtime," Hindemith's directions to the pianist derive straight from Stravinsky's playbook, in his desire to treat the piano as an "interesting type of percussion" and for the work to be performed "very wildly but in very strict rhythm." The movement is more authentically ragtime than similar efforts by Stravinsky, whose first exposure to jazz and rags came from sheet music rather than actual performance.

Given a conceptual kinship in this piece, and their broader neoclassical leanings, it is perhaps surprising that Hindemith did not return Stravinsky's admiration. In 1940, the two men were certainly close enough geographically:

in Massachusetts, Hindemith taught at the Tanglewood Summer Festival while Stravinsky lectured at Harvard. Hindemith later moved on to Yale, where he became a highly influential and respected teacher.

The caliber and character of both composers were indeed Ivy League, without becoming ivory tower. Both wanted their music to be widely admired and performed. Hindemith went so far as to write a series of works specifically intended for amateur players; Stravinsky's late pieces with piano are technically undemanding and many steps removed from the orchestral brilliance of his *Petrushka* suite. Despite the variety of all the works that were to come from their pens, both remained musically uncompromising to the end.

Today, while of the three composers Stravinsky remains the most "box office," wider audiences have decisively validated a core repertoire that has always attracted top performers. As new styles are promulgated in the 21st century and music charts the future through its past, the legacies of Stravinsky, Schoenberg and Hindemith have achieved an assured place in our cultural history.

Robert Rimm
Philadelphia, 1999

ROBERT RIMM, managing partner of Chronos Studios in Philadelphia, combines the disciplines of music and language as educator, pianist, writer and translator. He is author of an anthology of 19th- and 20th-century pianist/composers and his articles regularly appear in prominent music publications. Mr. Rimm is a graduate of the University of Pennsylvania.

Glossary
of French and German Terms

aber (etwas rascher), but (a little quicker)

allmählich etwas breiter werden, gradually
    becoming a little broader

allmählich zurückgehen, gradually receding

Anfangszeitmaß, opening tempo

attaquez chaque fois, attack each time

äußerst kurz, extremely short

beschleunigt, accelerated

bewegt(er), (more) moving, agitated

breit(er), broad(er)

Dämpfer, mute (damper pedal)

die Tasten tonlos niederdrücken, the piano keys
    depressed without sound

drängend, pressing forward

eher, sooner, earlier, rather

ein wenig belebter, a bit more animated

etwas, somewhat

excessivement court (et fort), excessively
    short (and loud)

fast ohne jede Verlangsamung, almost without
    any slowing down

feurig, fiery, passionate

fließend(er), (more) flowing

flüchtig(er), (more) fleeting

gebunden = legato

gedehnt, drawn out

genau im Takt, exactly in time

gesanglich, vocal

gut im Takt, quite in time

Hauptzeitmaß, the principal tempo, *tempo primo*

heftig, violent, forcible

hervortretend, prominent, to the fore

immer ruhiger werden, becoming more and more tranquil

im (ruhigen) Anfangszeitmaß, in the (serene)
    opening tempo

♩ *ist langsamer als die frühere* ♩
♩ is slower than the previous ♩

im Tempo = a tempo

laissez entendre bien nettement toutes les notes,
    let all the notes be heard quite clearly

laissez vibrer, let the sound ring

lang, long

langsam(er), slow(er)

langsame Viertel, slow quarter notes

langsames Walzertempo, slow waltz tempo

leicht, free

leise, slight, low [volume]

le nouveau très fort, the new [element] very loud

kaum hörbar, barely audible

kurz, short

mäßig(e), moderate

m.d., m.dr. [main droite] = R.H.

m.g. [main gauche] = L.H.

mit, with

mit Dämpfer, muted [with damper pedal]

mit Dämpfung (und Pedal) bis ⏀ , with damping
    (and pedal) until ⏀

mit sehr zartem Ausdruck, very gently expressive

mit Ton, with tone

moins fort, not so loud

nach und nach wieder schneller, once again faster,
    little by little

nach und nach in das Anfangszeitmaß
    (sehr rasche ♩ *) zurückkehrend*, reverting little by little
    to the opening tempo (very quick ♩)

nicht viel, not much

noch ruhiger, still calmer

Obertasten, upper keys

ohne = senza

rasch(er), quick(er)

♩. *rascher als die* ♩ *von früher*
♩. faster than the previous ♩

ruhig(er), calm(er)

sehr = molto

sehr ruhige Halbe, mit wenig Ausdruck, very calm
halves, with slight expression

schwungvoll, spirited

steigernd, wieder sehr rasch = crescendo, once more
very quick

très, very, *molto*
accentué, strongly accented
court, very short
fort, very loud

und, and

Untertasten, lower keys

viel langsamer, aber doch fließend, much slower,
but yet flowing

viel langsamer, als das I. Zeitmaß, much slower
than Tempo I

viel rascher, much livelier

viel schneller, much faster

voll, complete, full

weich, delicate, smooth, tender

wieder im Zeitmaß, once again in tempo

wie ein Hauch, like a breath

zart, subdued, gentle

(I.) Zeitmaß = Tempo I, *a tempo*

zögernd, hesitant

zurückhaltend, holding back

Longer footnotes and score notes:

p. 27

Sans changer le mouvement . . . par rapport au précédent.
Without changing the overall movement, the value of the
eighth [in 2/4] is the same as the eighth in the preceding
6/8. The marking "Più mosso" is meant only as an indication of the character of the new section as compared to
that of the preceding one.

p. 56

Répétez les sol♭ . . . doigts et ped.
Repeat the G-flats as smoothly as possible (*legato* of fingers
and pedal).

p. 85

steigernd (und beschleunigend) bis in ein ¢ *–Zeitmaß*
crescendo (and accelerating) up to a ¢ -tempo

p. 105

(dasselbe Zeitmaß . . . dieses Themas)
(the same tempo as in the very first appearance of this
theme)

p. 130

Nach jedem Stück . . . ineinander übergenhen!
Long pause after each piece. The pieces must not run
together!

p. 133

*In den ersten 4 Takten . . . durchaus **pp** spielen.*
In the first four measures, the right hand maintains a
continuous dynamic of *f*; the right, of ***pp***.

p. 138

The enigmatic "billboard"

5 Hutchinsons 5
Luft=Akt

refers to trapeze
artists—"The Five Hutchinsons"—who gave a vaudeville performance in the Schumann-Theater in Frankfurt. According to one
source, Hindemith is said to have composed the opening March
of his Suite during an aerial performance on September 4, 1921,
sketching his score on the back of his program. The word
Vorspiel at the opening of the March indicates a curtain-raiser
to the piece itself—a sort of three-measure overture.

p. 153

*Direction for use: Nimm keine Rücksichten . . . handele
dementsprechend.*
Pay no attention to what you learned in your piano lessons.
Don't stop to think about whether to play D-sharp with
your fourth or sixth finger.
Perform this piece very wildly, but in very strict rhythm
throughout, mechanically.
In this case, look on the piano as an interesting type of
percussion and proceed accordingly.

Twentieth-Century
Piano Classics

IGOR STRAVINSKY

Trois Mouvements de Pétrouchka
Rag Time • Piano-Rag-music
Les Cinq Doigts

Trois Mouvements de Pétrouchka

Three movements from Petrushka (1911) / Transcribed for solo piano by the composer (1921)

Edited by F. H. Schneider

I.

Русская • Danse russe • *Russian dance*

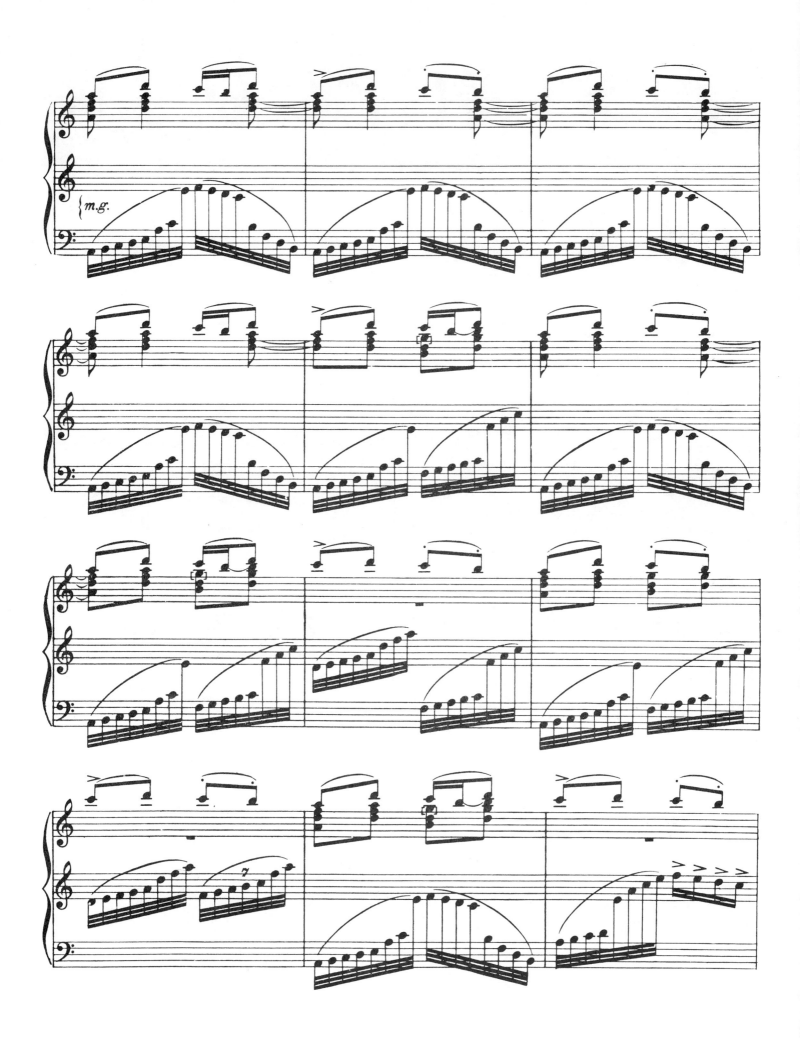

II.

У Петрушки • Chez Pétrouchka • *Petrushka's room*

*)8¨ äd libitum

III.
Масляница • La semaine grasse • *The Shrovetide fair*

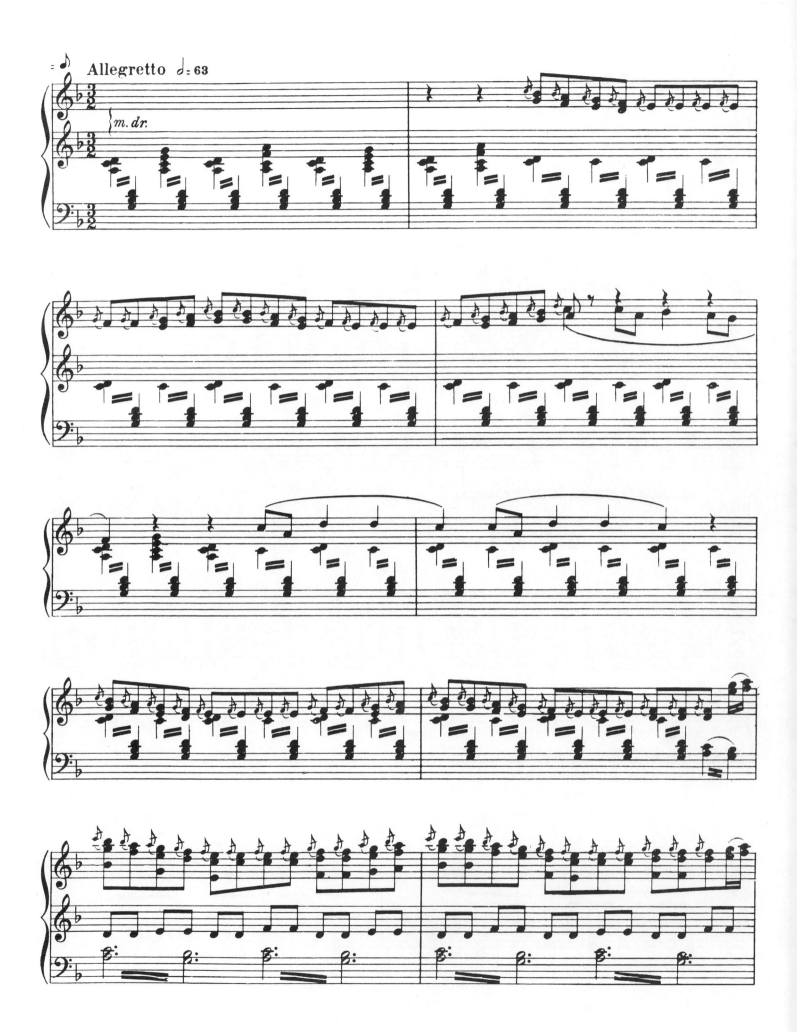

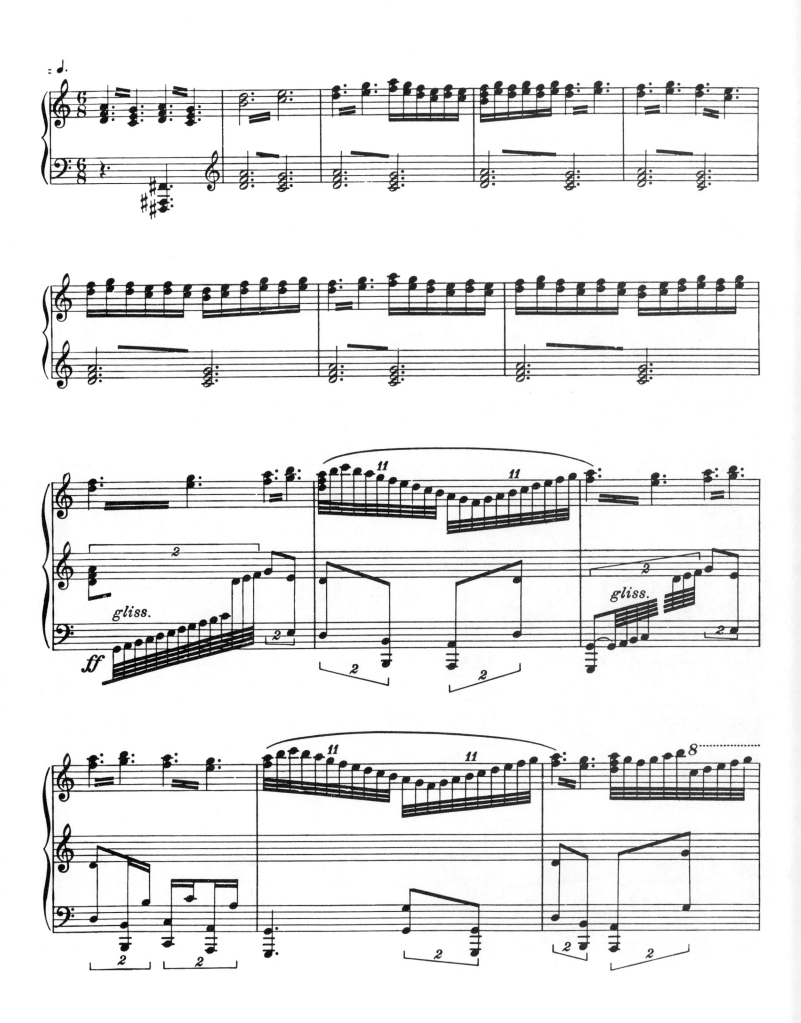

*) Sans changer le mouvement, la valeur de la ♪ étant la même que dans le 6/8 précédant. Le „Più mosso" n'est donc qu'une indication du caractère du mouvement par raport au précédant.

Rag Time

Music for eleven instruments (1918) / Transcribed for solo piano by the composer

Piano-Rag-music
(1919)

*) Répétez les sol ♭ de la façon la plus liée possible (legato des doigts et ped.)

Les Cinq Doigts
8 mélodies très faciles sur 5 notes
The Five Fingers: 8 very easy melodies on 5 notes (1921)

Andantino

Allegro

Allegretto

Larghetto

Moderato

Lento

Vivo

Pesante

Garches 1921

ARNOLD SCHOENBERG

Kammersymphonie, Op. 9
Drei Klavierstücke, Op. 11
Sechs kleine Klavierstücke, Op. 19

Kammersymphonie, Op. 9

[First] Chamber Symphony (for 15 solo instruments) (1906)

Transcribed for solo piano by Eduard Steuermann

22 **Sehr zart**

23

24 **Steigernd**

25 Hauptzeitmaß

zurückhaltend-   **26**

27 Fließend

28

steigernd und beschleunigend

nach und nach wieder schneller

50 Steigernd, wieder sehr rasch

51

64 nach und nach in das Anfangszeitmaß (sehr rasche ♩) zurückkehrend

accel.- - - - - -

sehr zurückhaltend

90 Schwungvoll
(dasselbe Zeitmaß wie beim ersten Auftreten dieses Themas)

ruhiger

Drei Klavierstücke, Op. 11

Three piano pieces (1909)

1.

2.

3.

Sechs kleine Klavierstücke, Op. 19

Six little piano pieces (1911)

I.

Nach jedem Stück ausgiebige Pause; die Stücke dürfen nicht ineinander übergehen!

II.

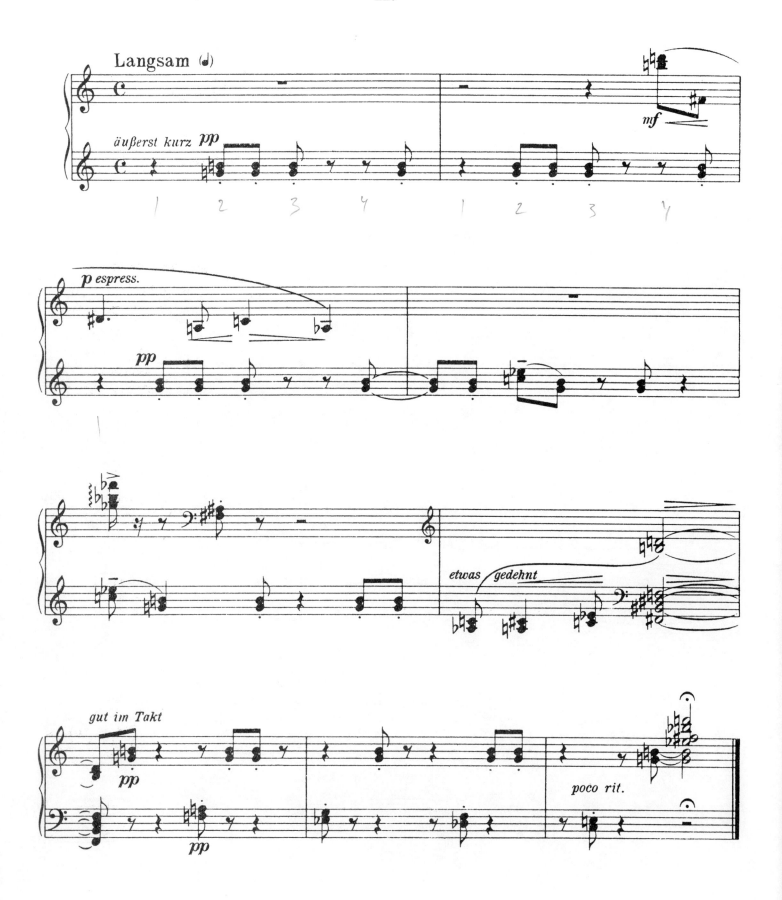

III.

Sehr langsame ♩

In den ersten 4 Takten soll die rechte Hand durchaus *f*, die linke durchaus *pp* spielen.

IV.

V.

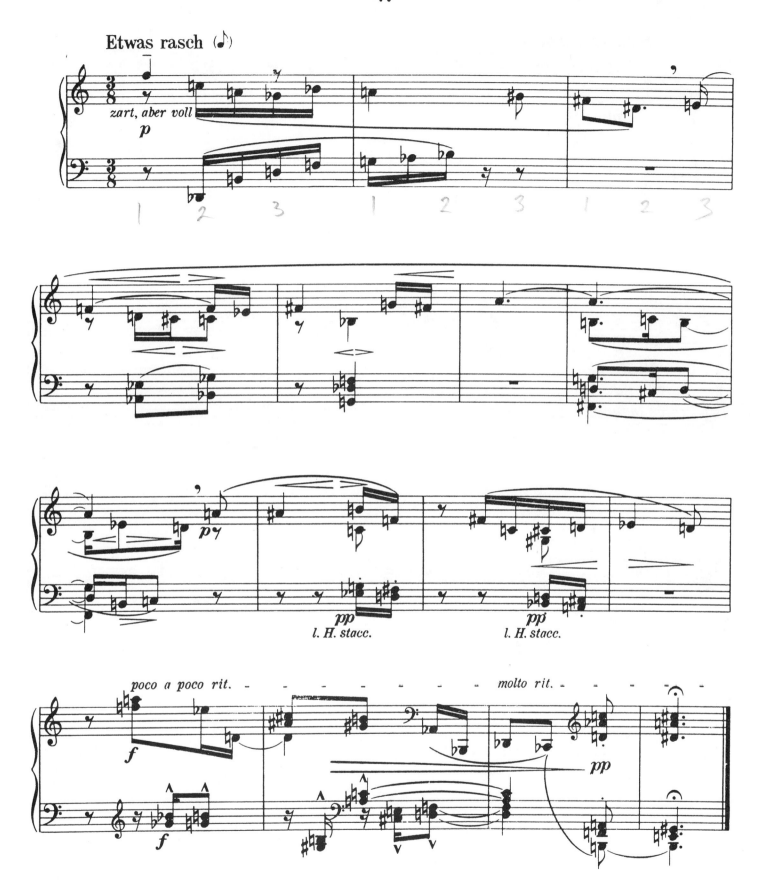

VI.

Sehr langsam (♩)

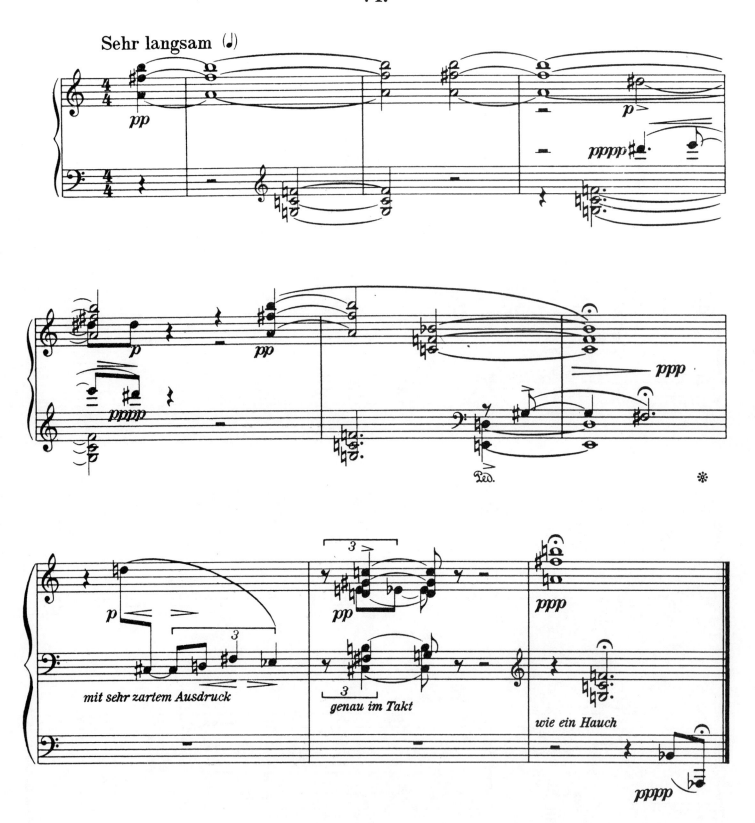

PAUL HINDEMITH

1922, Suite für Klavier, Op. 26

1922, Suite für Klavier, Op. 26
1922, Piano Suite

I. Marsch • *March*

II. Shimmy

III. Nachtstücke • *Night piece*

Sehr ruhige Halbe. Mit wenig Ausdruck.

IV. Boston

V. Ragtime

Mode d'emploi · Direction for Use

Nimm keine Rücksichten auf das, was Du in der Klavierstunde gelernt hast

Überlege nicht lange, ob Du *Dis* mit dem vierten oder sechsten Finger anschlagen mußt

Spiele dieses Stück sehr wild, aber stets sehr stramm im Rhythmus, wie eine Maschine

Betrachte hier das Klavier als eine interessante Art Schlagzeug und handele dementsprechend

Dover Piano and Keyboard Editions

THE WELL-TEMPERED CLAVIER: Books I and II, Complete, Johann Sebastian Bach. All 48 preludes and fugues in all major and minor keys. Authoritative Bach-Gesellschaft edition. Explanation of ornaments in English, tempo indications, music corrections. 208pp. 9⅜ × 12¼.
24532-2 Pa. **$9.95**

KEYBOARD MUSIC, J. S. Bach. Bach-Gesellschaft edition. For harpsichord, piano, other keyboard instruments. English Suites, French Suites, Six Partitas, Goldberg Variations, Two-Part Inventions, Three-Part Sinfonias. 312pp. 8⅛ × 11. 22360-4 Pa. **$12.95**

ITALIAN CONCERTO, CHROMATIC FANTASIA AND FUGUE AND OTHER WORKS FOR KEYBOARD, Johann Sebastian Bach. Sixteen of Bach's best-known, most-performed and most-recorded works for the keyboard, reproduced from the authoritative Bach-Gesellschaft edition. 112pp. 9 × 12. 25387-2 Pa. **$8.95**

COMPLETE KEYBOARD TRANSCRIPTIONS OF CONCERTOS BY BAROQUE COMPOSERS, Johann Sebastian Bach. Sixteen concertos by Vivaldi, Telemann and others, transcribed for solo keyboard instruments. Bach-Gesellschaft edition. 128pp. 9⅜ × 12¼.
25529-8 Pa. **$9.95**

ORGAN MUSIC, J. S. Bach. Bach-Gesellschaft edition. 93 works. 6 Trio Sonatas, German Organ Mass, Orgelbüchlein, Six Schubler Chorales, 18 Choral Preludes. 357pp. 8⅛ × 11. 22359-0 Pa. **$13.95**

COMPLETE PRELUDES AND FUGUES FOR ORGAN, Johann Sebastian Bach. All 25 of Bach's complete sets of preludes and fugues (i.e. compositions written as pairs), from the authoritative Bach-Gesellschaft edition. 168pp. 8⅜ × 11. 24816-X Pa. **$10.95**

TOCCATAS, FANTASIAS, PASSACAGLIA AND OTHER WORKS FOR ORGAN, J. S. Bach. Over 20 best-loved works including Toccata and Fugue in D Minor, BWV 565; Passacaglia and Fugue in C Minor, BWV 582, many more. Bach-Gesellschaft edition. 176pp. 9 × 12.
25403-8 Pa. **$10.95**

TWO- AND THREE-PART INVENTIONS, J. S. Bach. Reproduction of original autograph ms. Edited by Eric Simon. 62pp. 8⅛ × 11.
21982-8 Pa. **$8.95**

THE 36 FANTASIAS FOR KEYBOARD, Georg Philipp Telemann. Graceful compositions by 18th-century master. 1923 Breslauer edition. 80pp. 8⅛ × 11. 25365-1 Pa. **$6.95**

GREAT KEYBOARD SONATAS, Carl Philipp Emanuel Bach. Comprehensive two-volume edition contains 51 sonatas by second, most important son of Johann Sebastian Bach. Originality, rich harmony, delicate workmanship. Authoritative French edition. Total of 384pp. 8⅜ × 11¼.
Series I 24853-4 Pa. **$11.95**
Series II 24854-2 Pa. **$10.95**

KEYBOARD WORKS/Series One: Ordres I–XIII; Series Two: Ordres XIV–XXVII and Miscellaneous Pieces, François Couperin. Over 200 pieces. Reproduced directly from edition prepared by Johannes Brahms and Friedrich Chrysander. Total of 496pp. 8⅛ × 11.
Series I 25795-9 Pa. **$10.95**
Series II 25796-7 Pa. **$11.95**

KEYBOARD WORKS FOR SOLO INSTRUMENTS, G. F. Handel. 35 neglected works from Handel's vast oeuvre, originally jotted down as improvisations. Includes Eight Great Suites, others. New sequence. 174pp. 9⅜ × 12¼. 24338-9 Pa. **$10.95**

WORKS FOR ORGAN AND KEYBOARD, Jan Pieterszoon Sweelinck. Nearly all of early Dutch composer's difficult-to-find keyboard works. Chorale variations; toccatas, fantasias; variations on secular, dance tunes. Also, incomplete and/or modified works, plus fantasia by John Bull. 272pp. 9 × 12. 24935-2 Pa. **$14.95**

ORGAN WORKS, Dietrich Buxtehude. Complete organ works of extremely influential pre-Bach composer. Toccatas, preludes, chorales, more. Definitive Breitkopf & Härtel edition. 320pp. 8⅜ × 11¼. (Available in U.S. only) 25682-0 Pa. **$14.95**

THE FUGUES ON THE MAGNIFICAT FOR ORGAN OR KEYBOARD, Johann Pachelbel. 94 pieces representative of Pachelbel's magnificent contribution to keyboard composition; can be played on the organ, harpsichord or piano. 100pp. 9 × 12. (Available in U.S. only)
25037-7 Pa. **$8.95**

MY LADY NEVELLS BOOKE OF VIRGINAL MUSIC, William Byrd. 42 compositions in modern notation from 1591 ms. For any keyboard instrument. 245pp. 8⅛ × 11. 22246-2 Pa. **$13.95**

ELIZABETH ROGERS HIR VIRGINALL BOOKE, edited with calligraphy by Charles J. F. Cofone. All 112 pieces from noted 1656 manuscript, most never before published. Composers include Thomas Brewer, William Byrd, Orlando Gibbons, etc. 125pp. 9 × 12. 23138-0 Pa. **$10.95**

THE FITZWILLIAM VIRGINAL BOOK, edited by J. Fuller Maitland, W. B. Squire. Famous early 17th-century collection of keyboard music, 300 works by Morley, Byrd, Bull, Gibbons, etc. Modern notation. Total of 938pp. 8⅜ × 11. Two-vol. set. 21068-5, 21069-3 Pa. **$34.90**

GREAT KEYBOARD SONATAS, Series I and Series II, Domenico Scarlatti. 78 of the most popular sonatas reproduced from the G. Ricordi edition edited by Alessandro Longo. Total of 320pp. 8⅜ × 11¼.
Series I 24996-4 Pa. **$9.95**
Series II 25003-2 Pa. **$9.95**

COMPLETE PIANO SONATAS, Joseph Haydn. 52 sonatas reprinted from authoritative Breitkopf & Härtel edition. Extremely clear and readable; ample space for notes, analysis. 464pp. 9⅜ × 12¼. 24726-0 Pa. **$11.95**
24727-9 Pa. **$11.95**

BAGATELLES, RONDOS AND OTHER SHORTER WORKS FOR PIANO, Ludwig van Beethoven. Most popular and most performed shorter works, including Rondo a capriccio in G and Andante in F. Breitkopf & Härtel edition. 128pp. 9⅜ × 12¼. 25392-9 Pa. **$8.95**

COMPLETE VARIATIONS FOR SOLO PIANO, Ludwig van Beethoven. Contains all 21 sets of Beethoven's piano variations, including the extremely popular *Diabelli Variations, Op. 120.* 240pp. 9⅜ × 12¼.
25188-8 Pa. **$12.95**

COMPLETE PIANO SONATAS, Ludwig van Beethoven. All sonatas in fine Schenker edition, with fingering, analytical material. One of best modern editions. 615pp. 9 × 12. Two-vol. set. 23134-8, 23135-6 Pa. **$25.90**

COMPLETE SONATAS FOR PIANOFORTE SOLO, Franz Schubert. All 15 sonatas. Breitkopf and Härtel edition. 293pp. 9⅜ × 12¼.
22647-6 Pa. **$13.95**

DANCES FOR SOLO PIANO, Franz Schubert. Over 350 waltzes, minuets, landler, ecossaises, other charming, melodic dance compositions reprinted from the authoritative Breitkopf & Härtel edition. 192pp. 9⅜ × 12¼.
26107-7 Pa. **$11.95**

Available from your music dealer or write for ***free*** *Music Catalog to*
Dover Publications, Inc., Dept. MUBI, 31 East 2nd Street, Mineola, N.Y. 11501.

Dover Piano and Keyboard Editions

ORGAN WORKS, César Franck. Composer's best-known works for organ, including Six Pieces, Trois Pieces, and Trois Chorals. Oblong format for easy use at keyboard. Authoritative Durand edition. 208pp. 11⅜ × 8¼.
25517-4 Pa. **$13.95**

IBERIA AND ESPAÑA: Two Complete Works for Solo Piano, Isaac Albeniz. Spanish composer's greatest piano works in authoritative editions. Includes the popular "Tango." 192pp. 9 × 12.
25367-8 Pa. **$10.95**

GOYESCAS, SPANISH DANCES AND OTHER WORKS FOR SOLO PIANO, Enrique Granados. Great Spanish composer's most admired, most performed suites for the piano, in definitive Spanish editions. 176pp. 9 × 12.
25481-X Pa. **$9.95**

SELECTED PIANO COMPOSITIONS, César Franck, edited by Vincent d'Indy. Outstanding selection of influential French composer's piano works, including early pieces and the two masterpieces—Prelude, Choral and Fugue; and Prelude, Aria and Finale. Ten works in all. 138pp. 9 × 12.
23269-7 Pa. **$10.95**

THE COMPLETE PRELUDES AND ETUDES FOR PIANOFORTE SOLO, Alexander Scriabin. All the preludes and etudes including many perfectly spun miniatures. Edited by K. N. Igumnov and Y. I. Mil'shteyn. 250pp. 9 × 12.
22919-X Pa. **$11.95**

COMPLETE PIANO SONATAS, Alexander Scriabin. All ten of Scriabin's sonatas, reprinted from an authoritative early Russian edition. 256pp. 8⅜ × 11¼.
25850-5 Pa. **$12.95**

COMPLETE PRELUDES AND ETUDES-TABLEAUX, Serge Rachmaninoff. Forty-one of his greatest works for solo piano, including the riveting C Minor, G-Minor and B-Minor preludes, in authoritative editions. 208pp. 8⅜ × 11¼.
25696-0 Pa. **$11.95**

COMPLETE PIANO SONATAS, Sergei Prokofiev. Definitive Russian edition of nine sonatas (1907–1953), among the most important compositions in the modern piano repertoire. 288pp. 8⅜ × 11¼. (Available in U.S. only)
25689-8 Pa. **$12.95**

GYMNOPÉDIES, GNOSSIENNES AND OTHER WORKS FOR PIANO, Erik Satie. The largest Satie collection of piano works yet published, 17 in all, reprinted from the original French editions. 176pp. 9 × 12. (Not available in France or Germany)
25978-1 Pa. **$10.95**

TWENTY SHORT PIECES FOR PIANO (Sports et Divertissements), Erik Satie. French master's brilliant thumbnail sketches—verbal and musical–of various outdoor sports and amusements. English translations, 20 illustrations. Rare, limited 1925 edition. 48pp. 12 × 8⅞. (Not available in France or Germany)
24365-6 Pa. **$6.95**

COMPLETE PRELUDES, IMPROMPTUS AND VALSES-CAPRICES, Gabriel Fauré. Eighteen elegantly wrought piano works in authoritative editions. Only one-volume collection. 144pp. 9 × 12. (Not available in France or Germany)
25789-4 Pa. **$8.95**

PIANO MUSIC OF BÉLA BARTÓK, Series I, Béla Bartók. New, definitive Archive Edition incorporating composer's corrections. Includes *Funeral March* from *Kossuth, Fourteen Bagatelles,* Bartók's break to modernism. 167pp. 9 × 12. (Available in U.S. only)
24108-4 Pa. **$11.95**

PIANO MUSIC OF BÉLA BARTÓK, Series II, Béla Bartók. Second in the Archive Edition incorporating composer's corrections. 85 short pieces *For Children, Two Elegies, Two Romanian Dances,* etc. 192pp. 9 × 12. (Available in U.S. only)
24109-2 Pa. **$11.95**

FRENCH PIANO MUSIC, AN ANTHOLOGY, Isidor Phillipp (ed.). 44 complete works, 1670–1905, by Lully, Couperin, Rameau, Alkan, Saint-Saëns, Delibes, Bizet, Godard, many others; favorites, lesser-known examples, but all top quality. 188pp. 9 × 12. (Not available in France or Germany)
23381-2 Pa. **$12.95**

NINETEENTH-CENTURY EUROPEAN PIANO MUSIC: Unfamiliar Masterworks, John Gillespie (ed.). Difficult-to-find etudes, toccatas, polkas, impromptus, waltzes, etc., by Albéniz, Bizet, Chabrier, Fauré, Smetana, Richard Strauss, Wagner and 16 other composers. 62 pieces. 343pp. 9 × 12. (Not available in France or Germany)
23447-9 Pa. **$19.95**

RARE MASTERPIECES OF RUSSIAN PIANO MUSIC: Eleven Pieces by Glinka, Balakirev, Glazunov and Others, edited by Dmitry Feofanov. Glinka's *Prayer*, Balakirev's *Reverie*, Liapunov's *Transcendental Etude, Op. 11, No. 10,* and eight others–full, authoritative scores from Russian texts. 144pp. 9 × 12.
24659-0 Pa. **$9.95**

HUMORESQUES AND OTHER WORKS FOR SOLO PIANO, Antonín Dvořák. Humoresques, Op. 101, complete, Silhouettes, Op. 8, Poetic Tone Pictures, Theme with Variations, Op. 36, 4 Slavonic Dances, more. 160pp. 9 × 12.
28355-0 Pa. **$10.95**

PIANO MUSIC, Louis M. Gottschalk. 26 pieces (including covers) by early 19th-century American genius. "Bamboula," "The Banjo," other Creole, Negro-based material, through elegant salon music. 301pp. 9¼ × 12.
21683-7 Pa. **$15.95**

SOUSA'S GREAT MARCHES IN PIANO TRANSCRIPTION, John Philip Sousa. Playing edition includes: "The Stars and Stripes Forever," "King Cotton," "Washington Post," much more. 24 illustrations. 111pp. 9 × 12.
23132-1 Pa. **$7.95**

COMPLETE PIANO RAGS, Scott Joplin. All 38 piano rags by the acknowledged master of the form, reprinted from the publisher's original editions complete with sheet music covers. Introduction by David A. Jasen. 208pp. 9 × 12.
25807-6 Pa. **$9.95**

RAGTIME REDISCOVERIES, selected by Trebor Jay Tichenor. 64 unusual rags demonstrate diversity of style, local tradition. Original sheet music. 320pp. 9 × 12.
23776-1 Pa. **$14.95**

RAGTIME RARITIES, edited by Trebor Jay Tichenor. 63 tuneful, rediscovered piano rags by 51 composers (or teams). Does not duplicate selections in *Classic Piano Rags* (Dover, 20469-3). 305pp. 9 × 12.
23157-7 Pa. **$14.95**

CLASSIC PIANO RAGS, selected with an introduction by Rudi Blesh. Best ragtime music (1897–1922) by Scott Joplin, James Scott, Joseph F. Lamb, Tom Turpin, nine others. 364pp. 9 × 12. 20469-3 Pa. **$15.95**

RAGTIME GEMS: Original Sheet Music for 25 Ragtime Classics, edited by David A. Jasen. Includes original sheet music and covers for 25 rags, including three of Scott Joplin's finest: *Searchlight Rag, Rose Leaf Rag* and *Fig Leaf Rag.* 122pp. 9 × 12.
25248-5 Pa. **$8.95**

NOCTURNES AND BARCAROLLES FOR SOLO PIANO, Gabriel Fauré. 12 nocturnes and 12 barcarolles reprinted from authoritative French editions. 208pp. 9⅜ × 12¼. (Not available in France or Germany)
27955-3 Pa. **$12.95**

FAVORITE WALTZES, POLKAS AND OTHER DANCES FOR SOLO PIANO, Johann Strauss, Jr. Blue Danube, Tales from Vienna Woods, many other best-known waltzes and other dances. 160pp. 9 × 12.
27851-4 Pa. **$10.95**

SELECTED PIANO WORKS FOR FOUR HANDS, Franz Schubert. 24 separate pieces (16 most popular titles): Three Military Marches, Lebensstürme, Four Polonaises, Four Ländler, etc. Rehearsal numbers added. 273pp. 9 × 12.
23529-7 Pa. **$12.95**

---

*Available from your music dealer or write for **free** Music Catalog to*
Dover Publications, Inc., Dept. MUBI, 31 East 2nd Street, Mineola, N.Y. 11501.

Dover Orchestral Scores

THE SIX BRANDENBURG CONCERTOS AND THE FOUR ORCHESTRAL SUITES IN FULL SCORE, Johann Sebastian Bach. Complete standard Bach-Gesellschaft editions in large, clear format. Study score. 273pp. 9 × 12. 23376-6 Pa. **$11.95**

COMPLETE CONCERTI FOR SOLO KEYBOARD AND ORCHESTRA IN FULL SCORE, Johann Sebastian Bach. Bach's seven complete concerti for solo keyboard and orchestra in full score from the authoritative Bach-Gesellschaft edition. 206pp. 9 × 12. 24929-8 Pa. **$11.95**

THE THREE VIOLIN CONCERTI IN FULL SCORE, Johann Sebastian Bach. Concerto in A Minor, BWV 1041; Concerto in E Major, BWV 1042; and Concerto for Two Violins in D Minor, BWV 1043. Bach-Gesellschaft editions. 64pp. $9\frac{3}{8} \times 12\frac{1}{4}$. 25124-1 Pa. **$6.95**

GREAT ORGAN CONCERTI, OPP. 4 & 7, IN FULL SCORE, George Frideric Handel. 12 organ concerti composed by great Baroque master are reproduced in full score from the *Deutsche Handelgesellschaft* edition. 138pp. $9\frac{3}{8} \times 12\frac{1}{4}$. 24462-8 Pa. **$8.95**

COMPLETE CONCERTI GROSSI IN FULL SCORE, George Frideric Handel. Monumental Opus 6 Concerti Grossi, Opus 3 and "Alexander's Feast" Concerti Grossi–19 in all–reproduced from most authoritative edition. 258pp. $9\frac{3}{8} \times 12\frac{1}{4}$. 24187-4 Pa. **$13.95**

COMPLETE CONCERTI GROSSI IN FULL SCORE, Arcangelo Corelli. All 12 concerti in the famous late nineteenth-century edition prepared by violinist Joseph Joachim and musicologist Friedrich Chrysander. 240pp. $8\frac{3}{8} \times 11\frac{1}{4}$. 25606-5 Pa. **$12.95**

WATER MUSIC AND MUSIC FOR THE ROYAL FIREWORKS IN FULL SCORE, George Frideric Handel. Full scores of two of the most popular Baroque orchestral works performed today–reprinted from definitive Deutsche Handelgesellschaft edition. Todal of 96pp. $8\frac{5}{8} \times 11$. 25070-9 Pa. **$8.95**

LATER SYMPHONIES, Wolfgang Amadeus Mozart. Full orchestral scores to last symphonies (Nos. 35–41) reproduced from definitive Breitkopf & Härtel Complete Works edition. Study score. 285pp. 9 × 12. 23052-X Pa. **$12.95**

17 DIVERTIMENTI FOR VARIOUS INSTRUMENTS, Wolfgang Amadeus Mozart. Sparkling pieces of great vitality and brilliance from 1771–1779; consecutively numbered from 1 to 17. Reproduced from definitive Breitkopf & Härtel Complete Works edition. Study score. 241pp. $9\frac{5}{8} \times 12\frac{1}{4}$. 23862-8 Pa. **$13.95**

PIANO CONCERTOS NOS. 11–16 IN FULL SCORE, Wolfgang Amadeus Mozart. Authoritative Breitkopf & Härtel edition of six staples of the concerto repertoire, including Mozart's cadenzas for Nos. 12–16. 256pp. $9\frac{3}{8} \times 12\frac{1}{4}$. 25468-2 Pa. **$12.95**

PIANO CONCERTOS NOS. 17–22, Wolfgang Amadeus Mozart. Six complete piano concertos in full score, with Mozart's own cadenzas for Nos. 17–19. Breitkopf & Härtel edition. Study score. 370pp. $9\frac{3}{8} \times 12\frac{1}{4}$. 23599-8 Pa. **$16.95**

PIANO CONCERTOS NOS. 23–27, Wolfgang Amadeus Mozart. Mozart's last five piano concertos in full score, plus cadenzas for Nos. 23 and 27, and the Concert Rondo in D Major, K.382. Breitkopf & Härtel edition. Study score. 310pp. $9\frac{3}{8} \times 12\frac{1}{4}$. 23600-5 Pa. **$13.95**

CONCERTI FOR WIND INSTRUMENTS IN FULL SCORE, Wolfgang Amadeus Mozart. Exceptional volume contains ten pieces for orchestra and wind instruments and includes some of Mozart's finest, most popular music. 272pp. $9\frac{3}{8} \times 12\frac{1}{4}$. 25228-0 Pa. **$13.95**

THE VIOLIN CONCERTI AND THE SINFONIA CONCERTANTE, K.364, IN FULL SCORE, Wolfgang Amadeus Mozart. All five violin concerti and famed double concerto reproduced from authoritative Breitkopf & Härtel Complete Works Edition. 208pp. $9\frac{3}{8} \times 12\frac{1}{4}$. 25169-1 Pa. **$12.95**

SYMPHONIES 88–92 IN FULL SCORE: The Haydn Society Edition, Joseph Haydn. Full score of symphonies Nos. 88 through 92. Large, readable noteheads, ample margins for fingerings, etc., and extensive Editor's Commentary. 304pp. 9 × 12. (Available in U.S. only) 24445-8 Pa. **$15.95**

THE MAGIC FLUTE (DIE ZAUBERFLÖTE) IN FULL SCORE, Wolfgang Amadeus Mozart. Authoritative C. F. Peters edition of Mozart's last opera featuring all the spoken dialogue. Translation of German frontmatter. Dramatis personae. List of Numbers. 226pp. 9 × 12. 24783-X Pa. **$12.95**

FOUR SYMPHONIES IN FULL SCORE, Franz Schubert. Schubert's four most popular symphonies: No. 4 in C Minor ("Tragic"); No. 5 in B-flat Major; No. 8 in B Minor ("Unfinished"); and No. 9 in C Major ("Great"). Breitkopf & Härtel edition. Study score. 261pp. $9\frac{3}{8} \times 12\frac{1}{4}$. 23681-1 Pa. **$13.95**

GREAT OVERTURES IN FULL SCORE, Carl Maria von Weber. Overtures to *Oberon, Der Freischutz, Euryanthe* and *Preciosa* reprinted from authoritative Breitkopf & Härtel editions. 112pp. 9 × 12. 25225-6 Pa. **$9.95**

SYMPHONIES NOS. 1, 2, 3, AND 4 IN FULL SCORE, Ludwig van Beethoven. Republication of H. Litolff edition. 272pp. 9 × 12. 26033-X Pa. **$11.95**

SYMPHONIES NOS. 5, 6 AND 7 IN FULL SCORE, Ludwig van Beethoven. Republication of the H. Litolff edition. 272pp. 9 × 12. 26034-8 Pa. **$11.95**

SYMPHONIES NOS. 8 AND 9 IN FULL SCORE, Ludwig van Beethoven. Republication of the H. Litolff edition. 256pp. 9 × 12. 26035-6 Pa. **$11.95**

SIX GREAT OVERTURES IN FULL SCORE, Ludwig van Beethoven. Six staples of the orchestral repertoire from authoritative Breitkopf & Härtel edition. *Leonore Overtures,* Nos. 1–3; Overtures to *Coriolanus, Egmont, Fidelio.* 288pp. 9 × 12. 24789-9 Pa. **$13.95**

COMPLETE PIANO CONCERTOS IN FULL SCORE, Ludwig van Beethoven. Complete scores of five great Beethoven piano concertos, with all cadenzas as he wrote them, reproduced from authoritative Breitkopf & Härtel edition. New table of contents. 384pp. $9\frac{3}{8} \times 12\frac{1}{4}$. 24563-2 Pa. **$15.95**

GREAT ROMANTIC VIOLIN CONCERTI IN FULL SCORE, Ludwig van Beethoven, Felix Mendelssohn and Peter Ilyitch Tchaikovsky. The Beethoven Op. 61, Mendelssohn Op. 64 and Tchaikovsky Op. 35 concertos reprinted from the Breitkopf & Härtel editions. 224pp. 9 × 12. 24989-1 Pa. **$12.95**

MAJOR ORCHESTRAL WORKS IN FULL SCORE, Felix Mendelssohn. Generally considered to be Mendelssohn's finest orchestral works, here in one volume are: the complete *Midsummer Night's Dream; Hebrides Overture; Calm Sea and Prosperous Voyage Overture;* Symphony No. 3 in A ("Scottish"); and Symphony No. 4 in A ("Italian"). Breitkopf & Härtel edition. Study score. 406pp. 9 × 12. 23184-4 Pa. **$18.95**

COMPLETE SYMPHONIES, Johannes Brahms. Full orchestral scores. No. 1 in C Minor, Op. 68; No. 2 in D Major, Op. 73; No. 3 in F Major, Op. 90; and No. 4 in E Minor, Op. 98. Reproduced from definitive Vienna Gesellschaft der Musikfreunde edition. Study score. 344pp. 9 × 12. 23053-8 Pa. **$14.95**

*Available from your music dealer or write for **free** Music Catalog to Dover Publications, Inc., Dept. MUBI, 31 East 2nd Street, Mineola, N.Y. 11501.*